THIRTY-FIVE YEARS ON DEATH ROW

COURT ORDER IGNORED

OVER 21 YEARS

THE ROGER COLLINS STORY

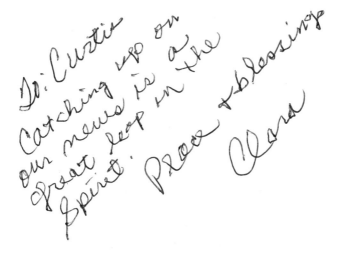

THIRTY-FIVE YEARS ON DEATH ROW

COURT ORDER IGNORED

OVER 21 YEARS

THE ROGER COLLINS STORY

AS TOLD TO

Clara Hunter King, Esq.

Printed and Bound in the United States of America
Published and Distributed by:
KINGDOM PUBLICATIONS
P. O. Box 360164
Decatur, GA 30036
(678) 412-2299
king.clara77@yahoo.com
www.kingdompublications.net
www.kp.moonfruit.com

An imprint of Professional Publishing House
1425 W. Manchester Avenue, Suite B
Los Angeles, CA 90047
(323) 750-3592
drrosie@aol.com
www.professionalpublishinghouse.com

Cover Design: Jay DeVance III
Formatting: Professional Publishing House

First printing, November 2012
ISBN: 978-0-9834299-7-5
Library of Congress Number: 2012922692

Roger Collins, 1977

Roger Collins, 2009

DEDICATION

This book is dedicated to all those who have family members, friends, or acquaintances locked up or tied up in the criminal justice system and those who agree that we *must* do something about our prison system.

Proverbs 31:8

Open your mouth for the speechless,
In the cause of all who are appointed to die
Open your mouth, judge righteously
And plead the cause of the poor and needy.

FOREWORD

I consider it an honor to write the foreword for *Thirty-five Years on Death Row: The Roger Collins Story.* This could have been my story. When I read Roger's story, I realized just how blessed my life has been. There have always been many people who cared about me. As a teenager, I got into trouble and ended up in jail. I turned my life around with help from my parents who stood by me. Roger didn't seem to have many people who cared about him or knew how to help him. Even if it seems that no one cares about you, you should care enough about yourself to hang with people that are making good choices.

Most young people don't know or care about the law. They just want to hang with their friends and have fun. All laws are made for a reason. If you violate the law, there is a penalty to be paid. When your friends ask you to do something that is against the law, they are asking you to take a chance on going to prison. You should say "No," immediately and without hesitation. You can still be their friend, just not the dummy friend.

If you end up in prison, you will be unhappy, homesick, and angry with yourself. But, you are not the only one that will be affected by your bad choices. It will affect your mother, father, brothers, sisters, grandmother, grandfather, cousins and friends. The word spreads when you end up in jail or prison. Everyone who cares about you feels the sadness and pain. After you have served your time in prison, your ability to get a job will be affected for years into the future. You will have a criminal record for the rest of your life. When you say "No" to a friend who asks you to do something that you know is a crime, you are not saying no to the friendship, just the prison time. If you go along because you want to keep the friendship, you will lose it when you end up behind bars. Your friends will not come to visit you, or write to you, or put money on the books for you. They will find new friends. Take it from someone who knows. I have been there, done that. I promise you; you don't want to go there. Learn to say "No" with a smile. Get in the mirror and practice if you have to. In the end, you will be glad you did.

Anthony E. King
Ramblings of a King

MESSAGE FROM THE STATE OF GEORGIA REGARDING THE DEATH PENALTY

To: Troy Davis

You have been convicted of murder
Because you killed someone
So, we are going to kill you
Because it's wrong to kill

To: Those gathered in a
vigil on the night of Troy's execution

Troy was sentenced to death for
Killing someone
So, we are going to kill him
And, we are ready, willing, and able
To kill you
If you try to stop us from killing him
Because it's wrong to kill

INTRODUCTION

This book was written for the specific purpose of helping young people make decisions that will keep them out of jails and prisons. It is based on the life of a man who is currently on death row. He has been scheduled for execution on three occasions, and the last "stay of execution" was granted six hours before his appointed time to die. This book will show you how to avoid the pitfalls that can land you in jail, in prison for life, or on death row.

Most young people get into trouble because they allow someone else to think for them and sometimes don't even realize that their behavior is a crime. Most of the time they know their behavior is a crime but follow along in an attempt to be cool or to impress their friends.

Statistics indicate that 1 out of 4 young men will serve time in prison during their lifetime. That means prisons are being built with you in mind. You can choose to accommodate them or keep them waiting. This book will provide you with the information you need to stay out of the system. It will provide parents with the information they need to help keep their children on the right path and avoid the heartache and sorrow experienced by parents whose children end up in jail, prison, and on death row.

After reading this book, you will know and understand when you should:

- Stop and ask questions
- Walk away
- Run and not look back

PART ONE

LIFE BEFORE PRISON
A TALE OF SURVIVAL

Roger died a little *on the inside* in 1977, as he entered Jackson State Prison in Jackson, Georgia. He was keenly aware of the fact that he was given a death sentence. He tried to prepare himself for his fate. As he was led into the prison, he stole a brief glance at everything he passed. It was his way of saying good-bye to inanimate objects because there would be no family or friends there to witness his last moments on earth. He felt alone, angry, confused, and helpless. His life was filled with pain, hunger, and fear. He relaxed a bit as he concluded that the pain and fear would end once and for all in a very short time. His feet felt like lead as he trudged down the long corridor. He took a deep breath and closed his eyes for just a second. In his mind, he could visualize the electric chair. He saw himself being strapped into the chair and waiting for the officer to step back and flip the switch. He purposed in his heart not to flinch, cry, or make any sound. He felt that he had to be a man, even in the end. He spent so much of his young life trying to be a man. But he didn't quite make it. In the end, he felt that he was still just an eighteen-year-old boy trying to act like a man. Everything in him wanted to scream, curse, beg them not to kill him, or try to get away. But he concluded that the end had come for him and tried to accept that fact. He knew the officers would not hesitate to use their weapons if he made one wrong move. "Since I have just a few more minutes left, don't rush it," he told himself.

Right from the beginning, Roger's life got off to a rocky start. His family was very poor and moved often. Roger was the only male, and he had five sisters. The Department of Family and Children Services records list the family income as $260.00 in 1974, and $114.00 in 1975. Roger failed both the second and third grades, and the school recommended that he be placed in a learning disability program. However, before that happened, his family moved again. He never got the special help he needed.

Roger was two years old when his mother, Lois, married his stepfather, Johnny Collins. That was the beginning of, what Roger describes as, a life of horror. His stepfather used drugs, alcohol, and was very abusive to Roger. He would come into Roger's room at night, place his hand over his mouth and nose and hold it until he sometimes passed out. At first, Roger thought it was a dream. He would awaken unable to breathe and struggled to free himself from the force holding him. After realizing it was his stepfather, he tried to avoid him.

Whenever his mother left the room, Roger always followed her. Roger was often stripped naked, tied to the bedpost and beaten until he was bloody. Sometimes he heard a noise and thought his mother was coming to stop it. She did not.

Roger was often denied food when his mother was not home. All the kids would gather around the table, and Johnny would give everyone food except Roger. One of his sisters would say, "Daddy, you didn't feed Man." Man is Roger's nickname. "Shut up and eat your food," Johnny would reply. Then Johnny would tell Roger to go outside and clean the yard. As Roger cleaned the yard, he always tried to figure out what he had done wrong that day. Johnny never told him what he did wrong. Later, Roger concluded that it was because Johnny wanted a boy so badly, and he had only girls. He could not figure out what to do about it, and there was no one to discuss it with. He learned to live with it.

When Roger overheard a conversation revealing the fact that Johnny was not his father and the name of his biological father, his heart filled with hope of finding his father and escaping his life of abuse, fear and hunger. He ran away from home in an attempt to find his father. He spent the night in the woods and pretended that his family was out looking for him. In his heart, he knew they were not. By the time he was eight years old, he became a chronic run-a-way. It was only when he came to the attention of the authorities that he was taken home or to the home of one of his aunts. However, he always ended up back in the clutches of his stepfather.

Then his mother told him that his father was married to another woman at the time of his conception. And, to make matters worse, she told him that his father asked her to abort him. Roger was devastated and his newfound dream of rescue from a terrible life was shattered. The sadness engulfed him like the darkness of the night, increasing his distrust of men.

When Roger was about eleven years old, Johnny led him and his foster brother on a series of thefts and robberies in Georgia and Florida. Johnny would talk with Roger and lay out the plans for the robbery. Roger began to feel a sense of belonging. It seemed as if Johnny actually needed him. Johnny always waited on the outside and took the money when they came out. Roger was forced to dress up as a girl and commit robberies. The police were looking for a young woman as the robbery suspect, but his family knew it was Roger. Several times Roger was arrested, and he took the fall and never told on Johnny. As he sat in his jail cell, he kept thinking that Johnny would come to visit him and thank him for not telling on him. It never happened. Roger describes, "Not being loved," as the most horrible feeling a child can experience.

Even today, Roger can still feel the pain from an incident in which he was totally humiliated by his own family and the police. Someone had burglarized a local store that belonged to one of the Church leaders. A relative convinced the family that it was Roger and one of his cousins.

"Tell the truth," the relative demanded. "If you don't, you will get a whipping for stealing and another one for lying." It was always best to confess to any accusation by a grownup, even if you didn't do it. The grownup always had the last say, and the child received two beatings if they didn't confess. They didn't need any real evidence, just an accusation by a grown up.

"We didn't," Roger and his cousin said in unison.

"If we find out you did it, you are in for two whippings," another relative said.

"We did it," his cousin said and Roger laughed. He always laughed when he was nervous. They had not burglarized the store, but knew that the relative that was trying to convince everyone would eventually succeed, and they would get two beatings if they didn't confess. However, this time when they confessed to burglarizing the store, it didn't help. Every grownup at the house beat them. Then they called the owner of the store and the police in an effort to scare them straight. The more nervous Roger became, the more he laughed. The police took ropes out of their vehicle and threatened to tie the rope around their necks and drag them down the street. His cousin was whimpering, and Roger kept laughing. He was too nervous to stop. The officers actually put ropes around their necks and tied them to the car. Then they got in the car and pretended that they would drag them up and down the street. Roger couldn't stop laughing. The relative was finally fed up with Roger.

"Take him to jail, since he thinks it's so funny," she said to the police officers.

They took Roger to jail, but did not put him in a cell. He was allowed to sit on a bench in the police station. The officers threatened Roger, called him names, and told him that they had hung his kind before. He felt alone, abandoned, and helpless, not knowing if he would ever make it home again. Not one grownup came to the police station to see if he was okay. After what seemed like hours to Roger, the officers took him home. The officers told his family that he cursed at them, and he received another beating. Roger was just glad he made it home alive.

When Roger left home at the age of eleven after a beating by Johnny, he had a severe injury to his arm but didn't realize that his arm was broken at the time. He felt the decision to leave was the only way he could survive. The beatings were becoming more frequent and more violent, and the entire family was in constant turmoil. Roger lived in constant fear. He was afraid even when Johnny was not home. So, he struck out on his own and nursed his arm until the pain finally eased. It was years later that he learned the arm had been broken. The doctor told him that it had healed incorrectly and needed to be broken again and reset to prevent constant problems in the future. The memory of the pain he suffered when his arm was broken caused Roger to say no to the doctors and take his chance on being able to deal with the pain in the future. Occasionally, he has pain in that arm, but he does not regret his choice.

Although Roger was happier living in the streets, he couldn't resist the "pull" on his young life to return to his home for long visits. He missed his mom and sisters. He often found them without food and electricity. Roger sold bottles, worked on fishing boats, picked tomatoes and oranges, and stole to help provide food for his family. His stepfather would start a fight with Roger's mom on Friday and leave home with his weekly pay and return "broke" on Sunday night.

Roger always came to his mother's defense when Johnny would beat her. A few times, he ran to call the police. He soon learned that it only made matters worse for everyone. Johnny would go into a rage and beat both Roger and his mother.

Roger only felt free and unafraid when he was hitchhiking or walking through the woods. He loved the woods, especially when it was raining. He would hide in the woods after running away from home, enjoying the illusion that everyone was worried and searching for him. He walked for miles in the woods and pretended he was the only person in the world. It made him feel very lonely, but it was a good kind of loneliness. The woods allowed him to close off thoughts of the abuse, hunger, and violence in his life. It seemed that most of his energy was spent trying to find something to eat and a place to sleep. There were times when he was lost and thought he would starve to death. He spent nights in laundry mats, abandoned houses and cars, the bus station, and in the back of nightclubs. Sometimes schoolmates would sneak him into their homes for a night, and he would sneak out before sunrise.

After leaving home, his school days were pretty much over. He hitchhiked from Florida to Georgia, for the first time, when he was just nine years old. He found people who were willing to give a kid a ride and not ask any questions. Some even gave him money. Then there were those who took him home with them and allowed him to spend the night.

In 1976, the violence within the family became nonstop. Johnny hit Lois in the head with an axe handle and tried to run her over with a car. As a result, she suffered serious injuries and a hearing loss. He stabbed her with a switchblade knife, and she defended herself by shooting him in the leg. This destroyed his calf muscle. The relationship finally ended in July after the couple engaged in a shootout at a nightclub where Lois worked. Lois was paralyzed from the waist down for several years and they both served time in jail.

A social worker made a home visit in July 1976 and found Roger taking care of his sisters, while Lois spent several weeks in the hospital before she was taken to jail. When she was released from jail, she was in a wheelchair and sent to a rehabilitation center. Lois was finally released from the rehab center in April 1977, and Roger went back to the streets.

Upon his release from jail, Johnny relocated to Florida. Roger breathed a sigh of relief. The violence was gone, the fear was gone, and he no longer lived in fear that his mother or sisters would be killed.

PART TWO

THE UNINTENDED SET-UP

Shortly after Lois Collins was released from rehab, and while she was still in a wheel chair, she met William "Bill" Durham. Bill was just six years older than Roger. Within a few weeks, he moved into the family home. Bill seemed so different from the other men Roger had known. Roger was angry and resentful toward all men until he met Bill. For the first time in his life, he felt that he had found a man he could trust. Bill bought Roger a car, secured a spot for him on the little league baseball team, and they spent a lot of time together. Bill was the first man who was nice to Roger and made him feel like he really counted.

Although Roger was not living in the home with his mother at the time, he came over often and Bill became the father figure he longed for. Roger felt he was on the road to becoming whole. His father had wanted him aborted, and his stepfather had abused him. He felt that someone had come into his life that would help him become a man. Roger tried to take a little piece of each man he met to determine his manhood prior to meeting Bill. He would observe the man from a distance and try to learn what he could about how to become a man. Bill treated him like a son, and it was a wonderful feeling. For the first time in his life, he was not constantly afraid and running. It seemed that he had spent his whole life running from something and never quite sure why he was running. Roger was constantly trying to impress Bill and obtain his approval. He wanted to be noticed and accepted. He wanted to show Bill that he could be a real man.

What seemed like the best thing that ever happened to Roger turned into a nightmare a few months after Bill moved into the family home.

Bill became a different person, and the family was plunged back into the same type of violence they were subjected to for so many years. Roger was disappointed, traumatized and confused by the behavior of the man he had come to think of as a real friend and father figure.

After the violence began, Bill kept a knife with him at all times. He slept with it under his pillow. He never tried to hide it, and it served as a constant threat when he physically abused Lois or her children. Roger decreased his visits to his mother's home. He no longer wanted to hang with Bill. But his mother wanted to keep the relationship going. Roger seemed so happy during the weeks before Bill turned violent and abusive. Lois seemed to be sure she could rekindle the relationship and make things right between her son and the man she thought would bring stability to his life.

Lois planned a barbecue, and Roger told her he would not be attending. She begged him to come by just to say hello to everyone.

In spite of the fact that Bill stood up in front of the group and yelled, "I love to kill, I love to kill, I love to kill," Lois begged Roger to go to the store with Bill to purchase beer. This was an attempt to rekindle the relationship between them. Roger refused to go to the store with Bill until J. C. Styles, Bill's first cousin, stated that he would go with them. Bill stated that he would drive the car. Although Roger didn't want to get into the car with Bill that night, he agreed to go in order to please his mother.

After purchasing beer and wine, they continued to drive around. They saw Delores Lester get out of a car and stopped to talk with her. Roger offered to give Delores a ride home, and she accepted and got into the car. Roger and Delores were boyfriend and girlfriend when they were much younger. For short periods of time, Delores lived in the house with Roger and his family. Roger knew her family well, had been in their home on many occasions, and had eaten meals with them. On a number of occasions, he took her mother home after finding her passed out from drinking. Once he heard someone crying and found Delores's mother in a ditch. It took him approximately thirty minutes to find a way to get her out of the ditch, before taking her home.

Roger's agreement to go to the store with Bill that night turned out to be a decision he will regret for the rest of his life. You see, a young woman lost her life that night through a senseless act of violence.

MORAL LESSON FOR YOUNG PEOPLE

When you learn that a person you trusted is not what they pretended to be, you must distance yourself from them. If that person is prone to violence and criminal activity, you must cut the relationship off no matter who wants to keep it going. This is an example of when it's time to "run, and not look back." Roger tried to make the right decision about Bill, but allowed his mother to persuade him to get in the car with Bill that night. When you override your "common sense" just to please someone else, no matter who they are, you will almost always regret it and you will be left to bear the consequences for your choice all by yourself. When you stand before the judge to hear the sentence imposed on you, all those who influenced you to make a bad choice will have moved on, or sit watching you from a "safe" place in the courtroom. Only your attorney will stand next to you. When it's over, he or she will walk away. This is the moment when it becomes so real to you that you could have made a better choice. By then, it's too late.

Although Bill was the leader and called all the shots that night, his cousin, J.C., twisted the facts because he knew the prosecutor would be seeking the death penalty. He wanted to be sure Roger was sentenced to death rather than his cousin. J.C. was also granted immunity for his testimony against Roger and Bill. Roger was on death row when he realized that Bill and J.C. were not his friends and that his mother did not always make the best choices for him. Roger will *never* forget that night. Thirty-five years is a long time to live in regret. Don't let it happen to you.

The thing that haunts Roger most about that night is that he didn't have the courage to try to stop the murder. He found himself walking in a daze. His actions that night were influenced by fear, misplaced loyalty, marijuana, and wine. At one time, he respected and admired Bill, now he was afraid of him, but he still wanted Bill to think of him as a man and in the midst of all that was happening, he somehow thought of Bill as a friend. The car Bill drove that night was the car that he purchased for Roger. Even though he drove recklessly and caused damage to the car, Roger didn't complain because Bill bought the car for him. Both Roger and Delores asked Bill to stop the car and let Delores out when he passed her house. He kept going. They stopped at a local store to get gas. Bill, Roger, and Delores went into the store. They purchased more beer and wine and a bottle of chocolate milk for Delores.

They continued to drive around and drink beer and smoke marijuana. Roger told Bill twice that he had to go home because he had to meet his girlfriend and take her kids home. Bill was in complete control and did not listen to anyone. He kept driving around and finally drove to a fenced-in wooded area off a dirt road. Roger did everything he could to fit in, and show Bill and J.C. that he was a real man. They took the backseats out of the car and placed them on the ground. They all engaged in sexual activity with Delores. Bill and Roger stated that it was consensual and J.C. said it was rape. Both Bill and J.C. testified that they had been intimate with Delores in the past.

BY ROGER COLLINS

"All three of us had too much to drink that night. We were all intoxicated. I was trying to fit in and act like one of the guys. Delores's death was a senseless act of violence due to Bill Durham's meanness and intoxication. It had nothing to do with rape.

"Someone suggested that we go to a party across town and we started in that direction. We stopped at a store and bought gas and more beer and wine. I asked Bill to take me home several times and to take Delores home. Even J.C. asked Bill to take Delores home. Bill ignored everyone and kept driving around in circles and then pulled off onto a dirt road and drove into a deserted field. We all got out of the car. There was no thought or talk about forced sex. No one had to rape Delores. She was not a bad person; she was a person who raised herself in the streets just as I did.

"When Bill took Delores by the hand and began to lead her toward the woods, I followed them. Bill turned around and told me to go get the jack out of the car. I didn't think. I just did what I was told to do. It never occurred to me that he would use the jack to kill Delores. After all, he had a long knife in his hand. If I had taken the jack as a murder weapon, I would have only taken the handle. I took the entire jack, and continued to follow. When I reached them, Delores was laying on the ground. She was not making a sound. I thought Bill had stabbed her with the knife. By that time I had figured out what he planned to do. I handed him the jack, turned and walked away. I heard the blows, but did not turn around and go back. I went back to the car and waited with J.C. I did not participate in the murder, but I am just as guilty because I made no attempt to stop it. I have struggled to forgive myself for what I didn't do that night. It may be that she would still be alive if I had done something to save her. Maybe if I had just walked away earlier it would have made a difference. Delores lived with us at one time, she was my girlfriend when we were much younger, and I would have never done anything to hurt her. My problem was that I didn't have the courage to stand up to Bill. I wanted to prove that I was a real man and that I could fit in. Somewhere down on the inside, I still thought of Bill as a friend.

"My priority and loyalty were in the wrong place. I did not rape Delores, nor did I actively participate in her murder. But I am guilty and deserve to be imprisoned because I did nothing to stop the murder. I could have done more than just asking him to take her home. I failed her, I failed her family, and I failed myself and my family.

"J.C. later admitted to his wife, Diane Styles, and his sister, Sarah Styles, that he lied on me and that I had nothing to do with the murder of Delores. He admitted that I was waiting by the car with him

49

when Bill came back with the bloody jack. His sister stated that she told my attorneys that J.C. admitted that he lied on me, but it took a long time to get the statement in writing. When they finally got back to her, she had been told not to speak with them again. J.C. lied when he testified that Bill and I raped Delores and that Bill forced him to rape her. He also lied and pretended that I was the leader and that I got Bill into killing. He wanted Bill to be punished for the murder, but he wanted me to get the death penalty rather than his cousin."

PART THREE

BEHIND THE SCENE: ARREST, TRIAL, AND APPEALS

J.C. went to the police the next morning, told them about the murder, and took them to the body. Both Roger and Durham were arrested on August 7, 1977.

Roger refused to talk with the police. But they were so friendly. They gave him cigarettes and coffee. They told him that they only wanted to help him, and they couldn't do that if he didn't tell them what happened. It was certainly a good feeling to have someone care about him and want to help him. Still, he hesitated. He had heard about how the police twisted what you say and used it against you. Then his mother and girlfriend were permitted to come in and talk with him. They both cried and begged Roger to talk with the police.

"Talk with them, they are just trying to help you," they repeated over and over, as they feverishly pleaded. Roger's mother testified at a post-trial hearing that she begged Roger to talk with the police because they told her that they were just trying to help him, but they would send Roger to prison without a trial if he didn't talk.

When Roger couldn't stand the begging and crying any longer, he agreed to talk with the police. During the initial interview, the officers told Roger that the conversation was being recorded. Then they came back on August 12, 1977 to interview him again and that conversation was also recorded. However, when the officers testified in court, they stated that the initial recording was not available. They said the recorder had malfunctioned. Roger stated that the police were faithful to their promise: Everything he said during that initial interview was used against him, and he swears that they changed the story completely. They testified as to what Roger said even though they did not take notes during the initial interview.

The officer testified that during the initial interview Roger said he raped and struck Delores with the jack. Roger stated that he said the sex was consensual, that only Bill struck Delores, and he never used the word rape.

MORAL LESSON FOR YOUNG PEOPLE

When the police tells you that everything you say *can* and *will* be used against you, take their word for it. Exercise your right to remain silent and talk with an attorney first. That way you avoid the risk of the officer saying you said something and you saying that's not what you said. People have a way of hearing and remembering things differently. You can avoid that by just keeping your mouth shut until you can speak with an attorney. That is your constitutional right; don't give it up. Tell them, "I'm exercising my right to remain silent. I don't want to talk until I have a chance to speak with an attorney." Then keep your mouth shut until you have spoken with an attorney. Even though you are telling the truth and have nothing to hide, wait and tell it to your attorney.

On December 22, 1982, one of Roger's attorneys filed an affidavit regarding a Brady Motion. A Brady Motion is filed with the court when an attorney withholds information that the law requires them to provide to the other attorney. The trial judge ordered the prosecutor to turn over all crime lab reports to Roger's attorneys. The affidavit states that Roger's clothes were tested for blood. The report came back negative, and the prosecutor did not provided this information to the defense attorney. Roger's attorney stated: "I feel that this crime lab report would have been helpful in Mr. Collins' trial and sentencing phase in that we would have argued that Mr. Collins was not close enough to the victim when the victim was struck to have committed the act personally."

Roger stated that he handed Bill the jack and walked away. Even though he had figured out what Bill planned to do, he didn't try to stop him. He knew that Bill had killed before, that was the reason he didn't want to go with Bill that night. Somehow he thought that J.C. would be a buffer, and he didn't want to disappoint his mother. In hindsight, he can see all the wrong choices, and lives with that every day.

When Roger came to his mom's house for the barbeque, he had his girlfriend's two small children with him. He left them with his mom when he went to the store with Bill and J.C.

Excerpts from J.C.'s testimony during the trial shows that Roger wanted to go home, but allowed himself to be dragged along when Bill ignored his request.

In the following excepts from the trial transcript, the defendants refer to the victim, Delores Luster, as Lois. Don't get her confused with Roger's mother, whose name is Lois Collins.

EXCERPTS FROM PAGES 145 TO 147 OF THE TRIAL TRANSCRIPT AT ROGER'S TRIAL

Cross Examination of J. C. Styles

Q   When was it that Mr. Collins told Mr. Durham that he had to get home?

A   Bill called him over to the side and they was talking.

Q   Now when was this?

A   That's when he had done knocked the muffler off the car. I could hear Roger tell him that he had to get home; he got to get home before his old lady do because he got to take those kids back.

Q   So he wanted to go home then?

A   Yes.

Q   Now let me ask you this, Mr. Styles: before you all got to this dirt road where the muffler was knocked off, isn't it a fact that Mr. Collins told Mr. Durham that why doesn't he just go ahead and take Miss Luster home?

A   That happened when he had pulled off from this motel, off from her house. Now he wanted to go home then, too.

Q   When was this?

A   When he left, when he left, coming back down Second Street to take her home, when Bill, he wanted to let her out then, too.

Q   Roger did, Mr. Collins?

A   Yes.

Q   That's the defendant here?

A   Right.

Q   And Bill just, Mr. Durham just kept going?

A   Yes.

Q   Didn't pay any attention to him?

A   No.

QUESTIONS

1. Why do you think Roger went along with Bill when he really wanted to go home?

2. What could Roger have done to avoid what happened to him that night?

3. At what point do you think Roger should have walked away?

MORAL LESSON FOR YOUNG PEOPLE

This testimony by J.C. clearly shows that Roger wanted to go home and wanted Bill to drop Delores off at her house. Bill ignored him. Roger didn't insist because he didn't want to make Bill angry. He also wanted to impress upon Bill and J.C. that he was a real man. If you continue to hang with friends who have no respect for the law, this could become your story. The individual who suggests the crime is often not the one who ends up in prison. The one who follows along to please that friend usually ends up in prison. Don't let it happen to you.

EXCERPTS FROM PAGES 113 TO 115 OF THE TRIAL TRANSCRIPT AT ROGER'S TRIAL

Direct Examination of J. C. Styles

Q   What did Bill say to the best of your knowledge, that you remember?

A   He said that it wasn't the first time that he killed; said killing come easy to him; said he killed, said he did a white girl like this.

Q   Did you ever see a weapon, John?

A   Yes.

Q   What kind of weapon was it?

A   A knife.

Q   What kind of a knife?

A   A white knife.

Q   Who had the knife?

A   Bill had it.

Q   When did you first see it?

A   I seen it when he come around to talk to
      me.

Q   How was he holding it?

A   He had it up on me just like this.

Q   Where was the blade pointing?

A   Pointed at me.

Q   John, I show you, it's marked State's
      Exhibit 10, can you identify this for me?

A   Yes.

Q   What is it?

A   It's the knife that Bill Durham had.

Q   Now when did he have it like this? Tell
      me.

A   When he was talking to me, telling me about the people he had killed and that he was going to kill Lois, and when I was talking to him trying to talk him out of it, looked like the more I talked to him the madder he'd get.

Q   What were you saying to him?

A   I told him that Lois wasn't worth getting into trouble about I know her, he know her and Roger know her. He said, "Well, we're going to…"

Q   And what was he doing with the knife?

A   He kept it on me and then he started to hit me with it but he stopped and he asked me, he said, "Can you keep your…mouth shut." I told him, "Yes, I can keep my mouth shut anytime."

Q   What was Roger doing when you were talking?

A   Roger, he was having sex with Lois.

Q   After you and Bill talked, what happened? What did y'all do?

A   Well, I started walking and Bill, he stayed back behind me, and when we got there, Roger, he was getting through, and he got up and Bill told me, said, "You're next."

Q   And what did you say?

A   I told him, "Hey, I don't want it. I don't care for it. I don't want to have sex with her, and he said—"

Q   Now, what—

A   I told him that I didn't want to have no sex with her; then he said, "I said we, we, we're going to…"

Q   When you say he who are you talking about?

A   Bill, Bill Durham.

Q   Now what was Lois doing?

A   Lois, she had been standing up at the time when Roger got through having sex with her.

Q   What was she saying or was she saying anything?

A   When we came back to Lois, when we approached Lois, that's when Lois started hollering.

Q   What was she hollering?

A   She was hollering, she was saying, "Why me; why me." She kept saying, "Why me."

Q   Now when you got to Lois what did you do?

A   When I got to Lois...

Q   What happened?

A   Bill told me, said. "Hey we' re going to..." and told me I was next.

Q   And what did you do?

A   I start pulling off my clothes; pulled off all my clothes.

QUESTIONS

1. Why do you think Bill told J.C that he had killed before?

2. Why do you think that Bill tried to force J.C. to rape the victim?

3. Do you think Bill would have harmed or killed J.C. if he refused to do as he was told?

4. Why do you think the victim started hollering, "Why me?" when Bill and J.C. approached her?

MORAL LESSON FOR YOUNG PEOPLE

J.C. agreed to go to the store with Bill because Roger refused to go alone. That decision affected the life of everyone in that car that night. Roger ended up on death row, Bill was given a life sentence, Delores lost her life, and J.C. had to live with his participation in that venture for the rest of his life. Sometimes your choice not to become involved in a venture or just to express your objection and walk away will turn the entire situation around. Don't ever go along with what you know is wrong to please someone else. If you end up in trouble and they have the opportunity to walk away, they won't think twice about leaving you. It happens all the time.

Watchdogs For Justice receive letters regularly from inmates who say they were the least culpable, and yet they received the harsher sentence. There were times when they didn't even know the crime had taken place. They waited in the car while someone went into a house or business to pick up something. They have been in prison for many years and filed many appeals. If you are with the individual(s) who commit a crime, you could end up in prison even if it seems that no one planned to commit a crime at the time you got together.

EXCERPTS FROM PAGES 202 TO 203 OF THE TRIAL TRANSCRIPT AT BILL DURHAM'S TRIAL

Cross examination of J.C. Styles

Q   Do you remember telling the police to begin with that Bill, that Roger Collins brought the jack out of the woods?

A   Yes.

Q   You told that to the police to begin with?

A   Yes, I told them that Roger brought it back.

Q   And now you are saying that Bill Durham brought it back?

A   Yes, I am.

Q   And you told the police then that you changed your mind about that; is that right?

A   Well, I didn't change my mind. I decided if I was going to tell anything, tell the truth on it, and he didn't.

Q   Are you saying you were lying then when you told the police first that Roger brought the jack out or are you lying now when you are telling us that Bill Durham brought the jack out?

A   I'm not lying. Bill brought the jack out.

Q   But you lied to the police to begin with; is that it?

A   No, I didn't lie, lie about it, no.

Q   You didn't?

A   No, not just to say I lied about it, no.

Q   But you did tell them that Roger brought the jack out of the woods, didn't you?

A   Yes.

Q   And was that the truth?

A   No.

Q   Well, it was a lie then, wasn't it?

A   Yes.

QUESTIONS

1. Why do you think J.C. told the police that Roger came out of the woods with the bloody jack when he knew it was Bill?

2. Do you think Roger believed that Bill and J.C. would lie on him to save each other?

   [ ] Yes   [ ] No

3. Do you have friends that you feel would lie on you to save a relative or another friend?

   [ ] Yes   [ ] no

4. If yes, do you still hang out with those friends?

   [ ] Yes   [ ] no

5. Is there anything about this story that will make you think twice about the individuals you hang with?

6. What do you feel was the worst decision
   Roger made that night?

7. What were some other mistakes he made?

These questions are included to show you how easily one can leave home with no intent of doing wrong and yet end up in a disastrous situation. Roger clearly intended to go back home. He intended to take his girlfriend's children back home. It has been thirty-five years now, and he has not yet made it back home. Several bad choices changed the course of his life forever. Don't let it happen to you.

I hope you will write your answers to the questions in this book and keep them for future reference. Also, I would love to know how you answered each question. If you don't mind sharing your answers with me, please go to my blog (www.35yearsondeathrow.wordpress.com)and post your answers. If you don't answer each question, please share the ones you answered on my blog and add any additional comment you may have. Your experiences and observations can help other young people stay on the right track. Thanks in advance for taking the time to post to my blog.

I would also like to have you visit WFJ's website at www.watchdogsforjustice.org.

MORAL LESSON FOR YOUNG PEOPLE

When reading the facts leading up to people being sentenced to death row and life in prison, many of them were continuously drinking alcoholic beverages and using drugs before the incident that lead to their criminal conviction. Roger, Bill, and J.C. were drinking beer, wine, and smoking marijuana before the crime occurred. Roger made a series of bad decisions.

#1 Getting into the car with Bill. When his mother begged him to go to the store with Bill, that was the time to say "No" and walk away.

#2 Not insisting that Bill stop and permit Delores to get out of the car when he passed her house. If he had, there would have been no charge of rape or murder.

#3 Not insisting that Bill take him back to his mother's house since he knew he was supposed to meet his girlfriend and take the two small children home.

Roger made a series of bad decisions in an effort to prove to Bill and J.C. that he was a man. But they didn't think twice about lying on him and trying to make him seem like the ringleader.

NOTE: Roger thought Bill was his friend, and his mother was trying to keep a relationship going that she thought was beneficial to him. Roger allowed them to think for him. If Roger had insisted that Bill take Delores home, he probably would have lost Bill's friendship. But that would have been a good thing because Bill turned out not to be a real friend anyway.

You need to make some decisions *before* you get into a car with a group of people.

- The first decision is to stop and ask questions. Where are we going? What are we going to do? Just riding around in a car full of people is the number one way young people eventually end up in trouble.

- The second decision should be that you will walk away if they decide to change the plans altogether and you can see it's going in the wrong direction.

- The third decision should be to run and not look back when someone *suggests* that you do something that you know is a crime.

If you don't make those types of decisions, the prison system is waiting for you. Every time someone asks you to do something criminal, they are asking you to take a chance on going to prison. It may seem hard to say no because you don't want to make them angry, or lose their friendship, or have them think you are not cool. Later, when you compare a sentence to prison for years, for life, or to death row, you will know that losing a friend, making someone angry or having someone think you are not cool would have been a far better choice.

In order to help you avoid this pitfall, I encourage you to get copies of our books *This is Not Cool: Volumes I & II*. The stories in these books are actual cases that Watchdogs for Justice members have handled in court. The stories show how young people leave home to have fun and hang with their friends, but one wrong decision changed their lives forever. Sometimes it's ten to twenty years before they return home. Sometimes they never make it back home. They end up in prison for life, on death row, or lose their lives. If you wait until you are in prison to make a better choice, it won't count. Make the right decision *before* you leave home. Sometimes the right decision may be not to even leave home.

I would like to share three letters written by students at King-Drew Magnet School in Los Angeles, California:

Dear Ms. King,

Thank you for speaking to our class. It was a great help to me. After listening to you, I went home and made a list of all the people that I call my friends. I realized how little I know about those people. As of now, I am getting some of those people out of my life because I realize they are not beneficial for me.

(Name withheld)

Dear Clara Hunter King,

I want to say thank you for coming to our school. In your book, This Is Not Cool, the story of Shontez is similar to a situation that happened to my brother. I wish he could have read that story before he got locked up. I just wanted to thank you for that.

Sincerely,
(Name withheld)

Dear Ms. King,

Thank you for coming to our school. It was a pleasure having you here. I was extremely glad to meet you because you are doing the exact job that I hope to have in the future. I am going to become a lawyer, but I hope to work with children.

My brother was one of those children who had problems. As of now, he is in jail for the rest of his life. I believe that this is because he didn't have that one person that told him his life could be better. If there is some small way I can be that person, I will have served my life's purpose. I am glad that there is someone else in the world who wants to make a difference. Thank you again, and God bless.

Sincerely,
(Name withheld)

PART FOUR

LIFE ON DEATH ROW

Roger is a very pleasant, easy-going person. If you saw him on the street or in a grocery store, you could easily imagine him to be a little league coach, a computer analyst or a high school PE teacher. However, his clothing tells the story about his occupation, or the lack of an occupation. He never really had an opportunity to choose an occupation. At the age of eighteen, he was found guilty of rape and murder by a Georgia jury and sentenced to death. He was illiterate, angry, and confused. When he walked into the prison, he expected to be executed that very same day. He was terrified and could barely put one foot in front of the other, as he trudged down the long hallway. The officers released him into a small, enclosed area and instructed him to go through to the next section. When he entered the next section, he came upon a chair, and he sat and waited for the officer to come and flip the switch. Another officer came into the room and told him that he was supposed to go through that area into G-cell area. A few days later, he was taken from his cell and to a room with a chair. He sat in the chair, as directed, and waited. He closed his eyes, as he waited for the officer to flip the switch. He opened his eyes when he felt something falling into his lap. He looked down, saw his hair falling all around him, and realized that he was in a barber's chair. He did not understand that he would not be executed right away. After his hair cut, he eventually ended up back in his cell. He still had no idea how much longer it would be before they came to take him to the electric chair.

For Roger, life in prison was pretty much the same as it had been on the outside. He seemed destined to spend his time upon this Earth fearful, angry and confused. He had no happy memories to replace the fear and hopelessness that overshadowed his thinking. He began to think of things he could do to occupy his mind. He decided that he needed to learn to read and write. Although he has a long way to go, and he is still working on his spelling, he now communicates regularly with family and friends by mail.

Roger has made many friends since entering prison. He has learned to trust more people while in prison than he ever did on the outside. He became a Christian, was baptized, and began attending church services in 1981. Prior to entering prison, he had never attended a Church service, and no one had ever told him that God loved him before. He has learned a lot since his imprisonment. His life has changed in so many positive ways.

Roger takes full responsibility for his action, or the lack of action, in the case and agrees that he deserves to be in prison. What he feels is so wrong, so unfair, and so unjust is the fact that his twenty-four-year-old stepfather was given a life sentence with the possibility of parole, while he, an eighteen-year-old, was given the death penalty. Everyone agreed that Bill was the ringleader.

At the sentencing hearing, the judge made the following statement regarding Bill Durham:

"My conclusion from the evidence is that as to the rape charge I think it is fair to conclude that but for his activities, but for this defendant's activities and his participation, the rape may never have occurred. The jury, of course, found that he is guilty of rape. The jury found Roger Collins guilty of rape. The undisputed testimony, at least, well, it's not undisputed, I grant you that this defendant disagrees with it, but there is evidence from which a fact-finder could decide, of course, that he attempted to cause another participant, co-defendant, if you will, to rape the girl, and so **I'm inclined to agree with the State** that as to the factual situation involving the assault on the girl, the rape on the girl, that this defendant would be properly characterized I think as the ringleader of that venture.

"I am not going to give him more than I did Roger Collins. However, in view of what I consider **his leadership role in the overall case**, I am going to follow the jury's recommendation and make it consecutive, and therefore, Mr. Durham, I'm going to sentence you to 15 years in the state penitentiary and run it consecutive to the life sentence you received in the murder case."

"So," you ask, "Why did Roger get a harsher sentence than Bill? Roger was only eighteen years old and Bill was twenty-four. Bill drove the car that night, he had the knife, he told J.C. he was going to kill the victim, he admitted that he had killed before, he came back to the car with the bloody murder weapon, and the judge and the prosecutor concluded that he was the ringleader. Shouldn't the sentence have been the other way around?"

ANSWER: Actually, this is the way the American criminal justice system seems to works. Too often, the individual who comes up with the idea or initiates the crime gets the least amount of time or no time at all. So, when you are with a group of people and one of them suggests you do something that you know is a crime and you go along with it, guess who is likely to get the most time. Hint: It will not be the person who made the suggestion. Most of the time, it will be the youngest, poorest, and least culpable individual in the group.

If the system worked the way it should **all the time**, we would always have:

- Honest police officers

- Impartial judges,

- Honest prosecutors

- Competent defense attorneys

- Honest expert witnesses

- Reasonable juries

- Dedicated justices that really review the relevant facts in each and every case, and apply the law to those facts.

If the system **never** worked the way it should, we would always have:

- Dishonest police officers

- Partial judges,

- Dishonest prosecutors

- Incompetent defense attorneys

- Dishonest expert witnesses

- Unreasonable juries

- Appellate courts justices that allow the law clerk to review the cases and write the opinion, and no one bothers to check to see if the cases used to uphold a verdict is still good law.

In reality, we have a system that is something in-between the two. Not everyone will receive justice and fairness in court. That's because the system is made up of people. And people come with a wide range of attitudes, beliefs, ideas and biases. Those attitudes are shaped by their experiences or the experiences of their family and friends, or others they have observed in the criminal justice system. Then there's the issue of whether they believe in redemption, or they have the ability to identify with the defendants or the victims. And to top it all off, the less money you have, the easier it is to convict you. So, if you are poor or very poor, you are more likely to be convicted than someone who has money. Do you think the county or state would have ignored an order to conduct a jury trial for a rich person for over twenty-one year? What about you, do you think they would treat you that way? You say, "I would make someone listen to me and take action on my behalf." That's exactly what Roger thought. And a lot of people tried to help him. It's not real clear what happened. It seems that there were never enough funds to make a difference. Remember, Roger was the youngest, poorest, and least culpable of the three. My advice to you is, "Don't take the chance." You should, "run and not look back" each and every time you see or hear anything that could possibly lead to you being arrested. If you get caught up in the system, you may never get out. Never!

Even if you are rich, don't take a chance on getting caught up in the system. Even for a short time, it's not a good place to be. It never adds anything good to your life.

Since his imprisonment, Roger has been scheduled for execution three times. He was granted a stay just six hours before the last scheduled execution.

On October 19, 1990, his attorneys filed a Writ of Habeas Corpus (A writ of habeas corpus directs a person, usually a prison warden, to bring the prisoner before the court in order to determine whether or not that person is imprisoned lawfully and whether or not he should be released from custody). The habeas filed on behalf of Roger contained eight claims.

The first claim states that it is unlawful to execute Roger because he is mentally retarded. Under Georgia law, it is unlawful to execute a person who is mentally retarded. The other claims detail violations of his constitutional rights after the arrest or during the trial.

As a result of the habeas, the following actions took place:

03-06-1991   The habeas court judge ordered a psychological examination to determine if Roger is mentally retarded.

03-18-1991   A psychologist examined Roger and filed his report with the court. According to the report, Roger had a full scale IQ of 66 (an IQ of 70 or below is considered mentally retarded.) The report further states: "Additionally, included in the evidence introduced against Mr. Collins were statements he made to the police. Based upon Mr. Collins' mental retardation, brain damage, inability to think abstractly, characteristic masking, and deference to authority figures, he would not have been able knowingly, voluntarily, and intelligently to waive his constitutional rights absent a painstaking and careful explanation of those rights."

03-18-1991   The habeas court judge signed an order and sent the case back to the trial court for a jury trial to determine if Roger is mentally retarded. The trial court is the court that held the original trial in 1977.

03-25-1991   The trial court judge sent a letter to the defense attorneys, prosecutors, and court clerk. He requested the entire case file from the habeas court. He also asked the attorneys if there was a time limitation for trying the case.

03-27-1991   The requested file was sent from the habeas court to the trial court.

04-02-1991   An attorney wrote to the trial court judge and stated: "With regard to your question regarding time limitations, there are none."

04-03-1991   An attorney wrote to the trial court's district attorney and stated: "There is no time period set for this trial to commence."

OVER TWENTY-ONE YEARS LATER

"So," you ask, "What happened **in the trial court** after April 3, 1991?" Nothing.

Roger, on the other hand, tried desperately to find an attorney to conduct the jury trial, and hearings on the seven additional claims.

Roger wrote to several well-known attorneys in Atlanta and several politicians and radio talk show hosts. Some responded with form letters, some referred him to other attorneys, and others did not respond at all.

In 1997 he wrote a letter "To Whom It May Concern" that was published in several newspapers. Two gentlemen from Ireland responded. They came to America to visit Roger. They met with Roger's family, the victim's family, and members of the jury that convicted Roger. In an article printed in *The Leinster Express*, on November 4, 2000, Mr. Colbert stated: "I have spoken to several of the jurors that convicted Collins and they have said to me that they never would have convicted him if the evidence known today had been available at the trial."

In 2000, Roger's friends from Ireland paid his mother's plane fare to Ireland so that she could help raise money for an appeal for him.

The Irish government was asked to admit Roger into their country on a parole basis and rehabilitate him. Roger's friends in Ireland organized, formed a protest, and wore t-shirts with Roger's name and picture on the front in their efforts to abolish the death penalty. They conducted raffles to raise money for his appeal. The death penalty has been abolished in Ireland.

Several attorneys have looked into Roger's case since that time. In 2010, an attorney made contact with a district attorney in an attempt to have Roger's sentence changed to life with the possibility of parole or to have him paroled to Ireland.

In September 2012, Roger asked our non-profit organization, Watchdogs for Justice, to contact the attorney general's office on his behalf. An attorney had also made contact with that office on his behalf in 2010. That office referred us to the trial court and the district attorney. We made contact with the district attorney on September 27, 2012. He responded immediately and asked us to contact his executive assistant to make an appointment. We made contact with his assistant, but the meeting never took place.

On October 5, 2012, we received a letter from Roger stating that an attorney visited him on September 26, 2012 and told him that the attorney that filed the habeas had agreed to handle his case. We informed the district attorney's office that we were no longer seeking a meeting on Roger's behalf.

We received a letter from Roger dated November 20, 2012 stating that the attorney met with the district attorney on November 2, 2012, and he has not yet heard how the meeting went. Also, he has not yet heard from the attorney that filed the habeas in 1991.

Roger is no longer seeking a jury trial on the mental retardation issue. The twenty-one-year delay has made it impossible for Roger to locate witnesses and maintain the evidence needed for a trial. To embark upon a trial after twenty one years would place him under a burden that he could never overcome. Therefore, he is asking the state and court to rectify this delay by commuting his sentence to life with the possibility of parole, the same sentence his co-defendant received.

If, by the grace of God, he is released from prison at some point, Roger vows that he will take all the good he has achieved in prison and leave all the bad behind. His hope is to marry and have a family. He would like to have children of his own. However, he says that a family can be a wife and a dog. His real passion is to operate a "cowboy ranch" for troubled teens. He feels that he is well qualified to do so. He wants to be able to house one hundred young men on his first ranch. He has plans to expand to as many states as possible.

He makes a point of reaching out to younger inmates who come to death row. He doesn't have many friends in prison and will always be grateful for the many friends he has on the outside. In addition to his friends in America, he has friends in Ireland, Germany, and France that correspond with him regularly. He says there are no words in the English language that can express his gratitude for his friends.

Roger is aware of the fact that his mother would have been upset with him had he walked away from her house that fateful night. He now realizes that her being upset cannot even be compared to what he has suffered as a result of being sent to prison. He is confined to a six-by-nine-foot cell twenty-three hours a day. He has no privacy. He was attacked by five other inmates and badly injured. As a result of the attack, he has had six surgeries on his right eye. Many of his family members have died and he has lost contact with some of them. Thirty-five years is a long time to maintain contact with someone behind bars.

"So," you ask, "What ever happened to Roger's father?" His father, Willie Thomas Lockett, died on his birthday, January 16, 1999. Roger never had a conversation with his father.

Roger felt hatred for his father since the day he learned that he asked to have him aborted. It was only after his death that he realized what he felt was hurt, abandonment, and need. The few times his father reached out to him, Roger resisted. His brothers and sister (on his father's side) wrote him in prison and informed him that they all knew about him and so did their mother. It was this information that made Roger realize that his father may not have been the kind of person he pictured him to be. He wonders what would have happened if he had gone to his father and told him about the abuse he suffered. He will never know if his father would have saved him from that situation. Because his mother told him about the request to abort him, Roger saw his father as the enemy just like every other adult. Once, when Roger was in Piggy Wiggly cleaning bottles he intended to sell, he saw his father walking toward him with two young children. His father spoke and held out a box of cookies to him. Roger ignored him, turned and left the store.

Now he realizes that his father may not have wanted him aborted at all, but was only thinking about his wife and children. After all, he was married and had a family when Lois told him she was pregnant, and Roger has no idea of the context of that conversation.

"Well," you ask, "What ever happened to his mother?" She died three days after his birthday on January 19, 2009.

She flew to Ireland in 2000 to help raise money for an appeal for Roger. That was a big deal for her. She was a country girl who had never been anywhere and was actually afraid of flying.

"I'll do it for *you*, Roger," was her declaration.

After that trip, she and Roger talked a lot and forgave each other. They became closer than they had ever been. Roger still finds it hard to believe that she is dead. He always loved his mother, even when he felt that she didn't love him. He didn't know how "not" to love his mother. He loved his sisters, aunts, and cousins. He didn't have the ability to care much for anyone else. His whole life before prison seemed to have been wrapped up in survival and maybe at some point getting a little bit of love or care from someone.

"And his stepfather," you ask, "What ever happened to him?"

Johnny moved to Florida and married another woman after he and Lois separated. He killed his new wife and was given a life sentence. He died in a Florida prison.

"So, what about J.C.?" you ask. An attorney traced J.C. to California and later to New York. He is reported to have died at age fifty while playing basketball in New York.

After Roger's friends from Ireland spoke with Delores's mother, Roger came to believe that she did not want to see Roger executed. However, he does not have any proof of that and she has since passed away. He feels that she would stand up for him if she was still alive. He must live with the fact that he failed to stand up for her daughter. He feels that she forgave him, and he has forgiven those who mistreated him over the years. Most importantly, he knows that God has forgiven him. He no longer hates himself, but he still struggles with forgiving himself. He comes closer every day. He has met and corresponded with so many wonderful people since his imprisonment. If he could have had a few of those people in his life as a young child, he would have been *then* who he is *now*. He knows that the blessings one receives were meant to be shared and passed on to others. In spite of all he has been through and the hurdles he must climb, he still maintains hope of being free one day. He vows that he will do everything in his power to help young men make decisions that will prevent them from traveling the road he traveled.

On April 24, 2003, Mr. Billy Colbert, of Portlaoise, Ireland spoke about the death penalty and Roger's case before the *Sub-Committee on Human Rights.* Following are excerpts from that speech:

"To execute somebody is an event, but the process of death row is one without measure. Its harvest is the death of many people and the families involved. We have sat with the three mothers involved, including the victim's mother. The word "generous" falls short to describe a woman who has opened her door in such circumstances. The community is predominantly black, but she has taken the risk despite orchestrated attempts on her estate to prevent her from communicating with three neighbours. The mother of the victim who was horrifically killed was also generous enough to open her door. The mother of the leading aggressive party also opened her door. These were moving experiences for Aiden O'Leary and me.

"Neither Mrs. Lester nor Mrs. Durham has sought the euphemism of closure towards Roger Collins. I would not have heard that if I had not been present. They do not seek revenge. As neighbours living

112

within 200 meters of each other, they understand this tragedy happened. The crime of Roger Collins is universally recognised as one of fear and stupidity. No human being has failed to be touched by fear and occasionally to a greater or lesser extent by stupidity. His crime took place when he was aged 17 and a half. He was overwhelmed by his mother's cohabiting partner. He is the only one of the three thus treated. This is a reflection of corruption, manipulation, trickery and deception in the process of the investigation and the prosecution."

When one of Roger's pen pals sent him the newspaper announcement about our Watchdogs for Justice Seminar in March 2011, Roger knew he had to contact us because we were doing just what he wanted to do: Teaching young people how to stay out of the system. I received a letter from him in May 2011 and visited him for the first time on July

27, 2011. I, along with Attorney Yvonne Hawks, have visited him a number of times since that date. We believe in redemption. We think he is an entirely different person than the angry, confused young man who was sent to death row thirty five years ago. We pray that one day he will be free and live out the plan God has for his life. There are many young people who need the direction and encouragement he can offer.

BY ROGER COLLINS

Roger wrote me a letter after the execution of Troy Davis. He stated:

"Troy Davis was put to death 20 minutes ago—we all feel so sad and I am thinking of his family. Why do we do some of the things we do to each other? Every execution takes something out of me. Mostly I feel rage and helplessness, but I am not broken. It makes me more determined to keep focused and move forward so that I can help keep as many young people as I can from coming to a place like this."

Roger was angry with God for a long time. He felt that no one was there for him when he was a helpless, abused child.

Not even God. He has come to realize that it was the grace of God that kept him through his horrible childhood. It's the grace of God that is keeping him while in prison. And he believes that the grace of God will set him free from prison and enable him to help others in a way no one ever helped him when he was a child.

MORAL LESSON FOR YOUNG PEOPLE

If you think you have it hard now, make sure you stay on the right side of the law. If you end up behind bars, it will be a whole lot worse. If you think your parents don't care about you because of their rules, you will think the prison personnel and officials hate you. If you are unhappy now, you will be most miserable in prison. So, instead of engaging in activity that can lead you down the wrong road, take steps to make your life better. If you are unhappy with your parents' rules, put forth your best effort to do well in school, get a good education, find a good job or start your own business and move out on your own. Don't leave home angry, just leave, and make your own way. Thank your parents for all they have done for you up to that point. After all, there was a time when you couldn't do anything but cry, drink formula, and create a need to have your pampers changed. Someone had to buy the pampers and the formula, and was there to love and comfort you when you cried.

Your own decisions will play a large part in how your future turns out. Even though Roger had a horrible childhood, his own choices to allow other people to think for him caused him to end up on death row. These were people that he felt cared about him. Remember, if the person makes poor choices for you, it doesn't matter if they care for your or not, the tragic results will be the same. Prison is real and "I wish I hadda" is a hard pill to swallow.

Roger has had help from many attorneys and friends. On several occasions, they have worked out a plan and everything seemed to be going along smoothly. Then without warning, the plans began to move in a different direction or there was a change in the attorneys and the process started all over again. Roger was always left with the choice of beginning again or giving up. The day he seriously considered giving up, it frightened him. Of all the things he has suffered, he had never considered giving up before. So he fought his way back to hope and started looking for help again. Roger cannot understand the reason things changed. However, he has become accustomed to such changes over the years. He has had to fight his way back to hope and start all over again, and again, and again. He knows he will succeed and one day he will be free because God has a purpose for his life. And it is not to stay in, or die in prison.

When I talked with Roger about how his childhood was basically stolen from him, this was his response:

"The way I lived my life cannot be justified— nor will I try to justify my wrong. But I think reasonable minded people can understand how I ended up as I was at that time. A boy must first learn what is right and proper. From that point on, he is accountable for his actions. My life and situation reflects so much evil, but I am as far from that person now as a man can be. The world may look on me as my stepfather did because they have failed to see my past through the eyes of the child I was. If people who judge me could see through the eyes of a child looking up at the only father he had ever known and see the horror of what was my reality, they would hug me instead of killing me."

MORAL LESSON FOR YOUNG PEOPLE

If you don't remember anything else from this book, don't forget this: Don't let anyone think for you. There are far more people in jails and prisons who allowed someone else to think for them than those who made bad choices on their own. In all your dealings with friends, family, and associates, make sure you evaluate each situation so that you can determine when it's time to:

- Stop and ask questions;
- Walk away, or;
- Run and not look back.

My prayer for you is that you come to realize that God has a plan and a purpose for your life. And it is not to sit in jail or prison. Maybe God's plan for you is to become a high school counselor, or an auto mechanic, or a doctor who discovers a cure for AIDS, or a barber, or a nurse who ministers to the sick, or a Sunday school teacher, or start your own business, or whatever it is you desire to do with your life. You have special talents and abilities that make you different from everyone else. If you don't know what your purpose is, think of what you really like doing. Think of what you would enjoy doing every day even if no one paid you. That may be your purpose for being on this Earth. And remember, you will never be truly successful until you find your purpose in life.

In Conclusion: Don't ever forget the options laid out for you in this book. Your freedom, and sometimes your very life, may depend on whether or not you make the right choice.

ORDER BOOKS BY CLARA HUNTER KING

QTY	Title	Unit Price	Total Price
	Justice On My Mind	$15.00	
	This Is Not Cool, Volume I	$10.00	
	This Is Not Cool, Volume II	$12.00	
	Departing This Life Preparations	$12.00	
	What You Need To Know Before You Start A Business	$15.00	
	What To Do Before You Get Hitched	$13.00	
	ABC's On How To Prpeare Your Manuscript For Editing, Formatting, And Printing	$10.00	
	How To Write A Book Made Simple	$13.00	
Cost of Books		$	
Shipping ($5.50 first book, $0.50 each additional book–call/email over 5 books)		$	
TOTAL		$	

MAKE CHECK PAYABLE AND MAIL TO:

Clara Hunter King
Attorney at Law
P. O. Box 360164, Decatur, GA 30036
(678) 412-2299

Name:_____

Address:_____

City:_____ State: _____ Zip: _____

Phone Number: (__) _____ Email:_____

Thank You!